Cars

KT-374-489

INTRODUCTION

i-SPY Cars covers a cross-section of cars seen on British roads, from popular mass-production models to high-performance supercars, off-roaders to people carriers and classics to ultra-modern hybrid electric cars.

Large manufacturers produce a great many models, so some cars could not be included because of space. New models are introduced throughout the year, so some will undoubtedly appear while you are still spotting those in our selection. Watch out too for model and maker names being different in different countries, for example cars badged as Vauxhall in the UK carry Opel badges elsewhere, while the Mitsubishi Shogun is named Pajero or Montero in most other countries.

We have selected photographs that will help you identify cars, then for each maker we give an impression of the model range and their place in today's car market. For the most part, we concentrate on current models – cars that are in production now, showing the latest developments in economy, safety and styling. It is important to remember the huge advances engineers have made in creating more fuel-efficient engines and hybrid powertrains that use both conventional and electric motors. Cars are also better than ever at protecting their occupants in a crash, thanks to stronger passenger compartments and numerous airbags.

Some cars exist for their performance and luxury – see the section towards the end of the book for the fastest and most glamorous cars on the road. Likewise, motoring heritage is valuable to many companies and classic cars are more popular than ever. They also have a separate section starting on page 60.

How to use your i-SPY book

Generally, cars appear in alphabetical order by manufacturer throughout the book, so they are easy to find. There are some exceptions to bring similar cars together especially in the supercars, luxury and classic cars sections. Score points for spotting any model in a family, not just the specific model shown in the picture. You need 1000 points to send off for your i-SPY certificate (see page 64) but that is not too difficult because there are masses of points in every book. Each entry has a star or circle and points value beside it. The stars represent harder to spot entries. As you make each i-SPY, write your score in the circle or star.

The ALFA (Anonima Lombarda Fabbrica Automobili) company was formed in 1910 and was changed to Alfa Romeo in 1920. In 1923 a young racing driver named Enzo Ferrari joined Alfa Romeo and would later run their racing team before leaving to design and manufacture cars under his own name. Both brands are now under the ownership of Fiat Chrysler. Often referred to as Alfa, they have a rich history in motor racing throughout the first part of the last century and have had victories in many races.

MiTo

Points: 10

GIULIETTA

Points: 10

GT

Points: 10

BRERA

Points: 10

lexan / Shutterstock.com

Roman Korotkov / Shutterstock.com

4C

Points: 20

Audi can trace its origin back to 1899 but became a major car producer when four German carmakers – Audi, Horch, DKW and Wanderer – merged to form Auto Union in 1932. It is now part of the Volkswagen Group along with other makes like Bentley, VW, Seat and Škoda and is seen as an upmarket and prestige brand. Like many manufacturers, Audi takes part in motor races with much success to advertise their brand, and in 2006 became the first company to win the Le Mans 24-hour race with a diesel-powered car. Look out for Audi's amazing R8 supercar that shares a platform and a V10 engine with the Lamborghini Gallardo. Take a special look at the Audi badge, with the four interlocking rings representing the four companies that merged to form Auto Union.

A3

Points: 5

Dmitry Eagle Orlov / Shutterstock.com

A4

Points: 5

AnnaMoskvina / Shutterstock.com

A5/A6/A7/A8
Score for any model from the Audi range of 'executive' saloons, and coupés.

Points: 10

Teddy Leung / Shutterstock.com

Mikhail Kolesnikov / Shutterstock.com

TT
Score double points if you find a diesel version.

Points: 10

Q3/Q5/Q7
Score for any of Audi's SUVs.

Points: 10

Younher_D / Shutterstock.com

30

belho rodrigues / Shutterstock.com

R8

Points: 30
Top Spot!

BMW – Bayerische Motoren Werke (Bavarian Motor Works) – was founded in 1916 primarily as a motorcycle and engine manufacturing company. After successfully making aircraft engines and motorcycles, BMW moved into car manufacturing and has had a remarkable transformation since the 1960s when it began to make high-quality mid-market saloons, as well as the luxury models it was known for. It now has the famous British names of Rolls-Royce and Mini within its group. Score double for any BMW with the blue and red M badge, denoting the high-performance version of a model.

1 SERIES/2 SERIES

The 2 Series is a coupé version of the 1 Series.

Points: 5

AnnaMariona / Shutterstock.com

3 SERIES/4 SERIES

The 4 Series is the coupé version of the 3 Series.

Points: 5

Volodymnna Kanzolyhs / Shutterstock.com

i3

Still hard to spot outside London, BMW's electric city car is one of the faster electric cars around.

Points: 20

X1/X3/X5/X6

The X range of SUVs increase in size as the number increases. Score for any of BMW's 4x4s, but double for the more scarce X6.

Points: 10

5 SERIES

Points: 5

6 SERIES

Points: 10

7 SERIES

Points: 10

Z4

Points: 15

Points: 35   **Top Spot!**   **i8**

Teddy Leung / Shutterstock.com

The highly innovative BMW i8 is a petrol-electric hybrid supercar that can go from 0–60 mph in just over four seconds. While electric cars become more commonplace on UK roads, spotting one of these electric supercars is still very rare.

Founded by André Citroën in France in 1919, Citroën was the first mass-production car manufacturer outside the USA. Citroën is famous for many technical innovations in their cars including clever systems using high-pressure fluid to run self-levelling suspension, steering and brakes. They are also famous for the 2CV *(see Classic Cars, page 60)* – a very simple, lightweight, two-cylinder car developed to bring affordable transport to rural France, but it was so successful, however, that it remained in production around the world from 1948 to 1990. Since 1976 Citroën has been part of PSA Group, Peugeot Citroën Automobiles based in Paris, and in 2015 it rebadged its luxury cars to a separate brand – DS Automobiles.

C-ZERO
Points: 15

C1/C3 POINTS: 5
Score for either hatchback.

C3 PICASSO/ C4 PICASSO
Score for any Picasso-badged MPV.

Points: 5

This Romanian firm has been owned by Renault since 1999 but it's only in more recent years that imports to the UK have risen sharply. Dacia offers some of the least expensive models in the UK and promotes their value for money.

SANDERO

Points: 10

LOGAN

Points: 15

DUSTER

Points: 10

The DS range are upmarket Citroëns, but they don't carry the Citroën name or even the double-chevron badge. The DS3 and DS4 share much with the Citroën C3 and C4, but the 5 is now a DS-only model.

DS3

Points: 10

DS4

The semi-SUV Crossback (shown) sits slightly higher than the standard model. Score for any DS4.

Points: 10

DS5

Points: 15

Fiat is an Italian manufacturer of all kinds of vehicles including cars and trucks, and is now amalgamated with Chrysler. It also owns Alfa Romeo, Maserati and Ferrari, and is heavily involved in motor racing, particularly Formula One. There was a very famous model called the Cinquecento or Fiat 500, a simple rear-engined runabout with a tiny 500cc engine that became very fashionable as a classic. The model was reinvented and its range has grown to include cars far larger than the original 500.

500 (NEW)
Score double points if you find a white one with green and red stripes. These are the colours of the Italian flag.

Points: 5

PANDA

Points: 10

PUNTO

Points: 10

500L MPW
A seven-seat MPV wearing the old 500's name badge.

Points: 20

QUBO/DOBLO
Score for either of Fiat's van-based MPVs.

Points: 10

The Ford Motor Company of America was started in 1903. Its founder, Henry Ford once famously said, 'You can have any colour of car you like, as long as it's black'. This remark referred to the company's famous Model T, which was the first mass market car produced on an assembly line, a method that was to transform the manufacture of cars. Henry Ford's vision changed car production forever and would be copied by all volume carmakers around the world. Today Ford has factories worldwide and has been in continuous family control for over 100 years.

KA

Points: 5

Art Konovalov / Shutterstock.com

FIESTA

Points: 5

Ed Aldridge / Shutterstock.com

FOCUS

Points: 5

Kurnyshov / Shutterstock.com

MONDEO

Points: 5

lexan / Shutterstock.com

B-MAX/C-MAX/S-MAX
Score for any of Ford's
MPV family.
Points: 10

EvrenKalinbacak / Shutterstock.com

MUSTANG
Ford's legendary muscle
car is now imported to the
UK in right-hand drive.

Points: 30
Top Spot!

Darren Brode / Shutterstock.com

Honda of Japan started life as motorcycle makers and still sell millions of motorcycles all over the world. In the 1960s they started to make small-engined motor cars – their first had chain driven rear wheels using almost the same technology used in motorcycles. Honda is relatively new as a maker, only starting manufacturing after World War II, and like others, has demonstrated its products through racing both motorcycles and cars in competitions, including Formula One.

JAZZ

Points: 5

CIVIC

Points: 5

HR-V/CR-V
Score for either of Honda's crossover SUVs.

Points: 10

Hyundai started life in the construction business in 1947 and became South Korea's largest industrial company. The Hyundai Motor Company's first global success came from their Pony model. It was particularly successful in the USA in the 1980s as American motorists came to value the economy offered by cars from the Far East.

i20

Points: 10

i40

Points: 10

SANTA FE/TUCSON
Score for either
Hyundai 4x4.

Points: 10

Nissan's luxury division started selling cars in America in 1989 but the marque's arrival in the UK and its home market, Japan, has been much more recent. Some models are now built in Nissan UK's plant in Sunderland, including the Q30 hatchback launched in late 2015 that should provide the bulk of Infiniti's European sales.

Q30

Points: 10

Q50/Q70
Score for either Infiniti saloon.

Points: 15

QX50/QX70
Score for either SUV.

Points: 20

Jaguar is a famous British marque with a long history of making sports cars and sporting saloons. Its most celebrated car was the E-type *(see Classic Cars, page 61)*, which every subsequent Jaguar sports car has had to live up to. The exciting F-type is the latest Jaguar to wear the E-type's crown, but the newest Jaguar – the F-PACE – is a daring move into the SUV market.

F-TYPE

Points: 15

XE/XF/XJ

Score for any of the four-door Jaguar saloons.

Points: 10

F-PACE

Points: 20

The first Jeep was a famous 4x4 vehicle chosen by the US Army to move quickly over difficult terrain. From the early days of military vehicles, the companies behind the Jeep brand – it's changed hands a few times – have used its reputation of strength and reliability to form the basis of an evermore refined range, though toughness and off-road prowess are still important. The vast majority of Jeeps are made for the USA market but Fiat Chrysler Automobiles, the brand's owner, imports models to Europe and the UK too.

RENEGADE

Points: 15

WRANGLER

Points: 10

CHEROKEE

Points: 10

Kia Motors is South Korea's second largest carmaker behind Hyundai. Founded in 1944 as a manufacturer of steel tubing and bicycles, Kia later went on to build motorcycles, trucks and cars. During the Asian financial crisis of 1997, Kia was sold to its rival Hyundai who have since sold part of the company but still remain involved in the business. In the past Kia have helped Mazda and Ford develop and produce cars for the local markets and this is a perfect example of how manufacturers who normally compete as rivals, cooperate with each other in order to enter certain markets and reduce their costs.

VENGA/CARENS
Score for either of Kia's MPVs.

Points: 10

Akimov Igor / Shutterstock.com

Zavatskiy Aleksandr / Shutterstock.com

SPORTAGE
Points: 5

lexan / Shutterstock.com

CEE'D/PRO_CEE'D
Score for any of this similar family of hatches and small estates.

Points: 10

Land Rover is probably the most famous off-road vehicle in the world. This British brand originated as a single, Jeep-like model developed by the Rover company, which finally stopped making cars in 2005. By then, Land Rover had been a separate business for some time, having developed more luxurious and versatile vehicles. Land Rover was bought by the Indian company, Tata Motors in 2008, along with Jaguar, and the basic Defender model that changed relatively little from the 1948 original only left production at the beginning of 2016.

RANGE ROVER
Score 15 for the sleeker Range Rover Sport.

Points: 10

Evren Kalinbacak / Shutterstock.com

Ed Aldridge / Shutterstock.com

DISCOVERY SPORT
Replacement for the popular Freelander model which was produced between 1997–2014.

 Points: 15

DISCOVERY

Points: 5

DEFENDER

Latest version of the 'original' Land Rover. Production stopped in 2016 but there are still many around.

Points: 15

RANGE ROVER EVOQUE

Points: 10

RANGE ROVER EVOQUE CONVERTIBLE

 Points: 25

Snap2Art / Shutterstock.com

TonyV3112 / Shutterstock.com

Steve Lagreca / Shutterstock.com

Lexus is the luxury brand of Toyota, and makes cars to compete with the other high-end companies like Mercedes, BMW and Audi. Lexus is a good example of a major manufacturer creating a new brand to compete in another segment of the market that they would not normally be able to enter. Score double points if you spot a car with an 'h' badge, indicating the hybrid power systems optional on most Lexus models.

LS

Points: 10

GS

Points: 10

CT

Points: 10

IS

Points: 10

RC-F

Points: 25

RX

Points: 15

Mazda is famous for using the Wankel rotary engine in its vehicles, first introduced in 1967 as a powerful, compact alternative to conventional piston engines. Other carmakers abandoned this design due to challenges with economy and reliability, but Mazda continued offering the Wankel until 2012.

Since the 1960s Ford has been involved with Mazda on many projects and now owns part of the Mazda Motor Corporation.

nitinut380 / Shutterstock.com

MAZDA2

Points: 10

Yauhen_D / Shutterstock.com

MAZDA3

Points: 10

Igor Polyakov / Shutterstock.com

MAZDA6

Points: 10

CX-3

Points: 10

CX-5

Points: 10

MX-5

Points: 15

MERCEDES-BENZ

Germany's Mercedes-Benz is one of the most prestigious carmakers in the world, with an instantly recognisable three-pointed star for a badge. The Mercedes AMG Petronas Formula One team won the World Championship for Constructors in 2014 and 2015. Today, Mercedes makes a vast range of cars from small upright city cars to vast, luxury 4x4s and sports coupés, plus everything in between. The AMG badge is equivalent to BMW's M badge: score double when you see this.

A-CLASS/B-CLASS
Score for either of these hatchbacks.

Points: 10

C-CLASS
Both this and the E-class have two-door coupé versions – score double for these.

Points: 10

E-CLASS

Points: 15

SL/SLK
Score for either of the two-seat Mercedes. The SL is the big brother.

Points: 15

CLA/CLS
Coupé equivalents of the C and E-class, but still with four doors. Also in estate form.

 Points: 15

S-CLASS

Points: 15

Points: 20

GLA/GLC/GLE/GLS/G

Yauhen_D / Shutterstock.com

HC-3889

Mercedes also have a range of chunky SUVs although they are not as familiar a sight on UK roads as their BMW or Audi equivalents. The GLA and GLC are at the smaller end of the range, while the GLE and GLS are more spacious. The permanently four-wheel drive G is a serious off-roader. Score for any Mercedes SUV.

The BMC Mini was first made in 1959 and was an instant hit. At the time it was revolutionary, adopting a new front-wheel drive engine and gearbox which was mounted transversely between the front wheels, enabling the car to be made smaller while remaining as roomy as previous models. The Mini has become iconic over the years and although now owned by Germany's BMW, the latest family of cars to wear a Mini badge is still made in Oxford. Look out for the designs that customise the Mini, many of which incorporate the Union Flag.

HATCH
Watch out for the Cooper models and special editions.

Points: 10

CLUBMAN
Points: 15

COUNTRYMAN
Score double if you see this or the Clubman parked next to the tiny original Mini.

 Points: 10

The Mitsubishi Company was founded in 1870 as a shipping firm, and car manufacture is just one part of this huge corporation. In 1970 the car company was formed and Chrysler, the US carmaker, has had an interest in the company almost from that time. Joint ventures with Hyundai of South Korea and Proton of Malaysia again illustrate the cooperation between carmakers in this global industry.

OUTLANDER
Score double for hybrid PHEV version.

Points: 10

ASX

Points: 10

SHOGUN

Points: 10

Nissan formerly sold cars under the Datsun name and was one of the first Japanese makers to sell cars in any volume in the UK with their small car, called the Datsun Cherry. Very quickly they established a good name in reliability and value for money they are one of the major global manufacturers and have a close alliance with the French car manufacturer, Renault.

MICRA

Points: 10

NOTE

Points: 5

LEAF

Points: 25

JUKE

Points: 10

OyuDang / Shutterstock.com

QASHQAI

Points: 10

Youhen_D / Shutterstock.com

X-TRAIL

Points: 10

FotograffF / Shutterstock.com

Darren Brode / Shutterstock.com

370Z

Points: 25

Peugeot's roots go back to a family business that was founded in 1810. In 1858 the Peugeot family filed its trademark lion and in 1889 produced its first automobile. Today Peugeot have a particular reputation in designing efficient diesel engines and have an excellent history in off-road rallying, including the famous Monte Carlo Rally. In 1976 Peugeot and Citroën merged into one company to form PSA Peugeot Citroën, based in Paris.

108

Points: 5

Zavatskiy Aleksandr / Shutterstock.com

208

Points: 5

Zavatskiy Aleksandr / Shutterstock.com

308

Points: 10

Grisha Bruev / Shutterstock.com

VanderWolf Images / Shutterstock.com

508

Points: 15

3008

Score the same for the 2008 hatch and 5008 MPV.

Points: 10

otomobil / Shutterstock.com

VanderWolf Images / Shutterstock.com

RCZ

Peugeot's take on the Audi TT concept has been a hit.

Points: 20

Founded in 1930 by Ferdinand Porsche, the company did not manufacture cars but was a consulting firm offering services to companies developing motor vehicles. One of the first tasks it undertook was on behalf of the German government to help develop a 'people's car' (in German: 'volks wagen') which resulted in the formation of the Volkswagen (VW) company and launch of their Beetle car. The first model under the Porsche name was the Porsche 64, produced in 1939 and using many of the same components as the VW Beetle. Porsche's most famous model, the 911, has been updated many times since 1963 but still retains the same overall shape and a rear-mounted, flat-six engine. More recently, Porsche has launched saloon and SUV models.

BOXSTER

Points: 15

Max Earey / Shutterstock.com

CAYMAN

Points: 25

Carccarofoto / Shutterstock.com

VanderWolf Images / Shutterstock.com

MACAN

Points: 20

Max Earey / Shutterstock.com

CAYENNE

Points: 10

Tadeas Skuhra / Shutterstock.com

PANAMERA

Points: 25

Points: 30   Top Spot!   **911**

30

Zavatskiy Aleksandr / Shutterstock.com

The 911 is one of the most iconic supercars of all time. The first model was built in 1963, and since then each new version of the 911 has managed to combine beautiful curved lines with blistering performance.

This combination has meant that the car is as well known for its success in rallying and track competition, as for its head turning ability on a country road or city street. Spotting one is always a pleasure.

The Renault brothers (Louis, Marcel and Fernand) together with two of their friends began producing cars in 1897 and sold their first Voiturette 1CV (meaning one horsepower) in 1898. Two years later the Renault Corporation was founded as 'Société Renault Frères'. They have been prominent in motor racing across Europe at the very highest levels, including Formula One. At the other end of the scale, a popular race championship for the Clio hatchback takes place in the UK.

TWIZY/ZOE

Renault's zero-emissions vehicles: Twizy is an eccentric micro-car, while ZOE looks like a traditional hatchback. Score for either.

Points: 20

TWINGO

Points: 10

CAPTUR

Points: 10

Vander/Wolf Images / Shutterstock.com

CLIO

Points: 5

Teddy Leung / Shutterstock.com

MÉGANE

Points: 5

Teddy Leung / Shutterstock.com

SCENIC/GRAND SCENIC

Points: 10

Rob Wilson / Shutterstock.com

SEAT (Sociedad Española de Automóviles de Turismo) was founded in Spain in 1950, initially with assistance from Group Fiat. The SEAT 600, based on the Fiat 600, was the first mass-produced car to be owned by many Spanish families. The collaboration with Fiat ended in 1981 and after producing cars independently, the company began a partnership with Audi/VW in 1986, which resulted in the integration of SEAT into the Volkswagen Group.

Dong liu / Shutterstock.com

IBIZA

Points: 5

LEON

Score double for the super-quick Cupra model.

Points: 5

Ed Aldridge / Shutterstock.com

ATECA

Points: 20

Maksim Toome / Shutterstock.com

Škoda is a car manufacturer based in the Czech Republic and became a subsidiary of the Volkswagen Group in 1991. The origins of Škoda go back to the mid-1890s when the company started out manufacturing bicycles. In 1899 their first motorcycle appeared and by 1905 the first car was produced. In 1924, after running into difficulties, they sought a partner and merged with Škoda Works, the biggest industrial enterprise in Czechoslovakia at the time, and adopted their name. They previously made unconventional 'no-frills' cars, but since the VW Group has taken them over they have enhanced their reputation and now appeal to many more customers.

FABIA

 Points: 10

YETI

 Points: 10

OCTAVIA

 Points: 5

SUPERB

 Points: 10

Unusually for a car company, smart began as a design concept shared between Mercedes and a watch brand, Swatch. Volkswagen took over backing at one point before Mercedes launched the first smart fortwo in 1998. The name comes from an abbreviation of **S**watch **M**ercedes **ART** and the company is part of Daimler AG, like Mercedes. This type of car is particularly suited to those living and travelling in cities as it is very short in length and can be parked very easily.

fortwo
Score double for a convertible.

Points: 10

forfour

Points: 15

roadster
Production stopped in the mid-2000s but a strong community of owners has kept a good number on the road.

Points: 30 Top Spot!

Subaru is a Japanese maker that first entered the UK market selling cars to those who needed to drive in off-road terrain or on muddy, unmade tracks. Typical customers included farmers and people living in remote parts of the country, but Subaru's four-wheel drive cars found much more success and credibility when the company turned to rallying, winning a total of five World Rally Championship titles. Subaru used to offer four-wheel drive with every model, but a recent venture into the joint production of a sporty two-door coupé with Toyota has ended this tradition with the arrival of the BRZ.

FORESTER

Points: 10

BRZ

Points: 20

OUTBACK

Points: 10

Suzuki was formed in 1909 to make weaving looms for the Japanese silk industry, and started making motor cars in 1937. After the end of World War II they developed small motorcycles as the demand for affordable transport grew in Japan. By 1952 Suzuki Motors was born. It is unusual for a motor company to start in cars, go on to motorcycles, and then back to cars. Today Suzuki is the ninth largest carmaker in the world as well as being one of the leading global motorcycle makers.

SWIFT

Points: 5

CELERIO

Points: 10

VITARA

Points: 5

Toyota is the largest motor car company in the world and has the luxury make Lexus in its family. In 1934 Toyota designed and built its first engine, followed in 1936 with the building of its first car. Toyota was another company to profit from the oil crisis in the US with increased sales of their economical smaller cars, which offered large fuel savings over the American cars of the day. This early success allowed Toyota to set up factories in America making cars designed specifically for the US domestic markets and also to build car plants in many other countries, including Britain.

AYGO

Points: 5

YARIS

Points: 10

PRIUS

Toyota's ground-breaking Prius is now much improved.

Points: 15

Zavodskiy Aleksandr / Shutterstock.com

AVENSIS

Points: 5

Vladimirs1984 / Shutterstock.com

LAND CRUISER

Points: 10

Souvoroff / Shutterstock.com

GT 86

Collaboration with Subaru, but with Toyota's own engine, not the Subaru flat-four.

Points: 20

Dong liu / Shutterstock.com

Vauxhall is a very old British marque, first making cars in 1903. Since 1925 it's been part of the General Motors Corporation but despite much model-sharing with German GM brand Opel, it's retained a strong British identity and manufacturing presence in Luton and Ellesmere Port, Cheshire. Vauxhall continues to enjoy strong sales to company fleet customers.

VIVA

An old Vauxhall model name is revived.

Points: 10

ADAM

Points: 10

CORSA

Points: 5

ASTRA

Points: 5

MERIVA/ZAFIRA

Score points for either of
Vauxhall's MPVs.

Points: 5

MOKKA

Points: 10

Volkswagen arose from a badly-bombed car factory that had started to produce a 'people's car' under the direction of the German Third Reich in the 1930s. German citizens were encouraged to invest a small sum every week to save for a new car, but the money largely disappeared and few were delivered. Post-war production was kick-started in Wolfsburg by a British Army Major called Ivan Hirst after UK manufacturers rejected the chance to acquire the tooling and build the car we would soon know as the Beetle. The rest of motoring history would be rather different if one of them had accepted, but in the 70 years since then, Volkswagen has become an immensely successful group with many famous marques under its control, including Bentley, Bugatti, Lamborghini, Audi, Seat and Škoda.

UP!

Points: 10

Fingerhut / Shutterstock.com

POLO

Points: 5

Teddy Leung / Shutterstock.com

GOLF/JETTA

Score double for the Golf-based saloon, the Jetta.

Points: 5

BEETLE (NEW)

Points: 15

PASSAT

Points: 5

TIGUAN/TOUAREG

Score for either of VW's SUVs.

Points: 10

Volvo is a Swedish carmaker with a strong reputation for making cars with excellent safety features. Like Saab, Volvo was very late in offering diesel engines in their cars due to the very cold conditions in their home market – diesel fuel can solidify in sub-zero Scandinavian winters. You will see many Volvo trucks on the roads that were originally part of the same company but are now independent following the sale of the car division to Ford in 2000. In 2010, Ford sold Volvo cars to a Chinese maker, Geely.

V40/V60/V90
Score for any hatchback or estate.

Points: 5

S60/S90
Score for either saloon.

Points: 10

XC60/XC90
Score for either crossover SUV.

Points: 10

ASTON MARTIN
James Bond's car of choice. Look out for sister luxury marque Lagonda's return from 2016.

Points: 20

BENTLEY
Hefty sports GTs and super-luxury saloons with a great British heritage, though now owned by VW.

Youzhen_D / Shutterstock.com

Points: 35
Top Spot!

Maksim Toome / Shutterstock.com

BUGATTI
Every part of the Chiron, Bugatti's latest supercar, is made as light as possible except for the solid silver Bugatti badge. That's why it has acceleration of 0–62mph in 2.5 seconds and a limited top speed of 261mph!

Points: 50
Top Spot!

FERRARI

Classic Italian sports cars founded by Enzo Ferrari in 1928 and are now part of the Fiat Group.

Points: 30
Top Spot!

LAMBORGHINI

Lamborghini produce some of the most powerful and expensive sports cars seen on the roads.

Points: 40
Top Spot!

LOTUS
British sports car manufacturer since 1952. Current models include the Elise and the Exige.

Points: 20

MASERATI
Range of luxury sports saloons and GTs benefiting from same ownership as Ferrari.

Points: 15

MCLAREN
F1 constructor now making road cars including the incredible 217mph P1.

Points: 40
Top Spot!

PAGANI

Out-doing Ferrari and Lamborghini for exclusivity, the Huayra costs £1.4 million.

Points: 40
Top Spot!

ROLLS-ROYCE

'The best car in the world' was once the slogan – could be true of modern R-Rs.

Points: 30
Top Spot!

STRETCHED LIMO

Mostly driven by chauffeurs as transport to parties and weddings. Many come with televisions, DVD players and bars as standard. Score double points for a pink one.

Points: 15

AC COBRA
Brutal machine created by putting an American Ford V8 engine into a light British sports car, the AC Ace. Score half if it's only a replica.

Points: 40
Top Spot!

BMC MINI
The original Mini was very popular so there are still quite a few around. Score double for one with a Union Jack on the roof.

Points: 20

CITROËN 2CV
Millions of these cheap and practical little cars were built between 1948 and 1990. In their day they were popular for their easy maintenance and soft ride, spotting them on UK roads is getting pretty difficult nowadays.

Points: 30   **Top Spot!**

FIAT 500 (ORIGINAL)
The original 'Cinquecento' (Italian for 500) was a tiny, twin-cylinder runabout that just about offered space for four.

Points: 25

FORD CAPRI
'The car you always promised yourself' said the advert, and the much-customised Capri became an object of desire for millions.

Points: 30 **Top Spot!**

JAGUAR E-TYPE
Enzo Ferrari called it the most beautiful car in the world – quite a recommendation! Score for either roadster or coupé versions.

Points: 25

MGB

Britain's most popular classic sports car? It lasted in production for nearly 20 years and thousands are still on the road.

Points: 20

MORRIS MINOR

The Minor was a huge post-war success story and the first British car to sell a million. Score double for a convertible or the cute, wood-framed Traveller.

Points: 30
Top Spot!

VW BEETLE (ORIGINAL)

The Beetle (or 'Bug' in North America, 'Käfer' in Germany) was an even greater success story than the Morris Minor. Score double for a convertible or a rare 'split screen' version.

 Points: 15

INDEX

i-SPY

How to get your i-SPY certificate and badge

Let us know when you've become a super-spotter with 1000 points and we'll send you a special certificate and badge!

HERE'S WHAT TO DO!

- ✓ Ask an adult to check your score.

- ✓ Visit www.collins.co.uk/i-SPY to apply for your certificate. If you are under the age of 13 you will need a parent or guardian to do this.

- ✓ We'll send your certificate via email and you'll receive a brilliant badge through the post!